THE MINI HANDBOOK

A Guide to the Infinite Within
Course and Workbook

Lamont P. McPheron
2019

3rd Edition published April 2019.
© 2014, 2015, 2019 Lamont P. McPheron
© 2019 art by Jai Lynn and Vicki Ramsay
Book design by Lotus Head Publishing
ISBN-13: 978-1-7337214-0-0
ISBN-10: 1-7337214-0-1

Integrated Mindfulness Institute
www.imi.earth

Dedicated to my radiant wife,
my two wondrous daughters,
my two talented step sons,
and to my father who taught me courage.
I'd also like to give a shout out to Dara, Daishon, Laya
and Sam.
We are all in this together.

Table of Contents

This handbook is a result of 25 years of dedicated practice and study in the field of mindfulness. Through my training in tai chi, meditation, yoga and chanting I've realized that my level of happiness is directly related to my overall level of mindfulness. I feel a responsibility to my culture to share what I have learned. My various diagrams and theories are meant to assist the reader in deepening their personal understanding of what mindfulness is and why it is profoundly effective at enhancing mental wellness. The workbook section was created to help the reader heighten his or her personal level of mindfulness.

I wish to acknowledge the instructors that I've been fortunate enough to work with. Bob Xu (tai chi), Jim Young (raja yoga), Santicaro (meditation), Sister Johanna Suebert (mysticism), and Dr. Steven Bennish (psychology), have all played significant roles in my overall education. My appreciation goes out to them for all their insight and energy.

The mind is the foundation of all human achievement. If you desire to improve your circumstances and your society, first improve your mind. Walk the walk of awareness. Let clarity be your new companion.

Chapter One
The Beginning

A New Way of Being

Awakening
To the Power
Of our Minds

Consciously Rewiring
and
Improving the Physical Structure of our Brains

Finding Internal Peace
In the process
Of Growth

The Mind

The mind is an amazing instrument. Its' power is immense. Through mindfulness training we can learn to harness this power. In doing so, we learn to be the conscious creator of our lives.

Think of your mind as a potent manifesting machine. Look around at every human-made object and realize that it originated from the human mind. Indeed, we are incredible beings. We are creators. Our minds are the foundation of this ability.

By patiently practicing mindfulness, we slowly learn to be the director of our minds. We can develop the clarity to understand our individual purpose and the skill to stay firmly on our unique path. Through training our minds, we develop the focus, insight and power required to achieve our potential.

A Solid Strategy

If We Want to Improve Our Circumstances
A Solid Strategy is to
Improve the Functioning
Of our Minds

Why Mindfulness?

The big question is, do you want to tap in to the vast power of your minds' latent potential? Do you want to fully understand your purpose and willfully create your life? If this is appealing, begin by applying your will to read this book. Complete the workbook as well. If you are beginning on this path, you will likely notice that life becomes more effortless. Duties, chores, and relationships will simply begin to flow. Your self-image will begin to deepen as a soulful perspective emerges. A sense of freedom will permeate your being as you let go of the overbearing future and the clinging past. Life will feel altogether lighter...

It takes courage to change. If you choose to train in mindfulness, you will break free of old patterns of thinking that perhaps have been passed down from generation to generation. While treading the mindful path, you will learn to elevate your mental habits. You will clearly realize that the pain of stagnation is far worse than the pain of growth. Perhaps it will soon be time for you to transform old stagnant and destructive mind patterns into productive habits of thinking and awareness.

I suggest viewing an overall mindful perspective as a type of empowering philosophy or lifestyle. From this perspective, success stems from finding balance between the analyzing (thinking) and the stillness (awareness) mind states, (see chapter 3). This is the place of equanimity. This type of balance leads to profound advancement in all areas of our life. Take the leap from stagnation to empowerment. A vibrant life awaits. Begin the journey of mindful living and be the witness to your personal transformation.

This Book

An Instruction Manual
For
Getting into
The Flow

Mindfulness – A Fresh Perspective

Mindfulness is a state of mind that transcends analytical thought. It is a place of full on awareness – beyond thinking. It is to be fully connected with the moment. It is the place of vital aliveness. It is the state of simply being.

We were all born mindful. We were present. For most of us, our minds were quiet and aware.

However, as we grew up we lost our quiet minds. Because of the intense and continual training of the analytical portion of our minds, many of us have lost the ability to find stillness. Compulsive thinking is the norm in our culture. This compulsive thinking leads to anxiety, depression, excessive anger, insomnia etc...

If we lack inner peace, we suffer. Many of us look in all the wrong places to find this "peace of mind". We are trained to believe that money, status, drugs, and stuff in general will bring us internal peace. However, through mindful living, we can find this peace of mind regardless of all the stuff. Also, when we find this internal peace, it enables us to live in such a way that brings us the stuff that we really do need to be fulfilled. In other words, finding internal stillness empowers us to successfully navigate through this complex culture, to a life of material success and meaning.

Mindful living is a philosophy that takes mindfulness to the next level. It entails using a variety of utilitarian mindfulness skills throughout the day and night. It is the way of habitual introspection and internal stillness. It enables us to see the world through fresh eyes and with an open and discerning mind. For many of us, it is a new way of being.

This is a path for those who desire to significantly shift their thinking and behavioral patterns. This is a path for those who are willing to seriously train and study.

Essentially, it is learning how to be in the flow state as much as possible. *To be in the flow often, leads to mental wellbeing.* Some of us get there naturally. However, for the rest of us, it takes perseverance, patience and a good lesson plan, (which I hope this book provides).

Carl Rogers, father of Person Centered Therapy, was a proponent of fully connecting with the moment. According to Rogers, "living each moment fully, not distorting the moment..." is one key to our mental wellbeing. In other words, he is suggesting that seeing each moment clearly and without prejudice is psychologically beneficial. Indeed, to be mindful is to *connect with the unbiased reality of the moment,* which is an effective and healthy place to be.

In fact, mindfulness can be viewed as a psychological prerequisite for mental health. To be non-judgmentally present, (mindful), naturally leads to a vital perspective. This vitality in turn leads to feelings of inspiration, love and intrinsic meaning. On a very basic level, to be fully present in the moment is to feel fully alive and connected to the flow. On the other hand, if we lack in present moment awareness, we tend to feel disconnected from the moment and this leads to depression and anxiety.

We each have an *innate drive* to have moments of full on awareness. If we are unable to achieve present moment awareness in a healthy manner, we may use unhealthy methods to get there. Substance abuse, overeating, and self-cutting behavior can be viewed as unhealthy methods of achieving a connection with the present moment. Being conscious of this phenomenon empowers us to substitute healthy mindfulness methods for unhealthy behaviors. Indeed, mindfulness practice treats the *source* rather than the *symptoms* of mental health dysfunction.

An Important Question

Where do you Spend Most of Your Time?
In the Past?
Or in the Future?
Or in the Present Moment?

It is Wise to Learn from the Past
And to have Goals for the Future

However

To Spend Much of our Time
Present and Connected
To this Moment

Vastly
Reduces
Our Stress

While Enhancing
Our Mental
Wellbeing

Chapter Two
Cultural Reality

Mindfulness in the Modern Culture

"The Mental Diet"

We live in the information age. Never before has the human mind been subjected to such a vast and relentless onslaught of information. This "information overload" causes mental agitation. This is a significant mental health issue in our culture but for the most part is widely ignored. We need to learn how to successfully manage our "mental diets" to achieve optimal mental wellness.

While engaging with various forms of screen time, the mind is busy ingesting and processing information. Also, after disengaging from the digital matrix, (such as turning off the TV), the mind continues to process the ingested information. Personally, I know if I spend too much time on Facebook, afterwards my mind feels stunned and dull. If I'm engaging in a Facebook debate, my mind tends to ponder it even long after I'm off the screen. Sometimes in the middle of the night my mind continues to evaluate the Facebook drama that is unfolding.

In our western culture, many of our minds are significantly occupied and disturbed by this information overload. In general, our minds tend to be very cluttered.

From a mindfulness perspective, all this mental clutter does not leave much room for moments of full on awareness.

Screen time can be seen as an alternative reality. This alternative reality is designed to be alluring and can be a place of solace, drama and excitement for millions of people. The experience of digitized reality can be very appealing - and addictive. That is why it is important to pay attention to both the quantity and quality of your screen time. Attempt to view the information that your mind ingests, (your "mental diet"), as crucial to your mental well-being.

Take an honest look at your "mental diet". Attempt to avoid "mental junk food". Also, push back against excessive habitual usage! Find moderation in the amount of digitized information your mind is ingesting. Be choosey with your "mental diet". This is a crucial variable in the equation of your mental wellness in this modern world.

The Modern Culture

The Information Age
Is upon us
Be choosey with
Your "Mental Diet"

Pay Attention
To What and How Much
You Feed Your Mind

Find Moderation

A Cluttered Mind
Is a Breeding Ground
For Confusion And
Agitation

A Clear Mind
Trends Towards Peace
And Inspiration

The Media Fast

Unplug yourself from the media matrix. Go on a "media fast". Try it out for a week and see how this benefits your overall clarity and emotional well-being. It is harder than you may think but very worthwhile.

I once asked a Tibetan meditation master if TV was poisonous for the mind. He replied, "No, the problem is that the TV clutters the mind and therefore makes meditation more difficult." If you are serious about mindfulness, give a "media fast" a try and you will be pleased with the results.

This is a rigorous trial. Avoid TV, the radio, internet news, social media, video games, billboards and even corporate ads on clothing. To achieve success in a "media fast" is difficult and may take some practice. However, it is a worthwhile endeavor. This is a cleanse for the mind.

I suggest attempting to go on a media fast every few months. Even a day away from the media is helpful for decluttering your mind. Also, be flexible with your media fast. For example, if it doesn't seem practical to completely avoid Facebook, just limit it. Perhaps only check it once a day and refuse to scroll down your page. Tailor your media fast to your own needs. Just pushing back on the onslaught of information that the mass media presents to us daily is a great mindfulness practice in itself!

Peace

The World is Peaceful
Floating in Space
Rotating Slowly
Gracefully

Drugs

Drugs, (including alcohol), can be appealing because these substances assist the mind in opening, relaxing, or focusing. Basically, downers such as alcohol and opioids help to relax the mind, while uppers such as cocaine and caffeine help the mind to stay focused and energized. Psychedelics can assist with opening the mind to new possibilities.

However, the drug-induced experience is short lived, not reliable and filled with side effects. Repeated compulsive usage is common. For example, if we become reliant on alcohol to relax, we may become dependent on it. The drug itself can have power over us. This is true of all drugs. To be addicted to any drug is to lack freedom.

Mindfulness can play a profound role in assisting us to find moderation with substances. By realizing that we have the power to relax, focus, and open our mind through mindfulness, the drugs have much less power over us. We also begin to understand that we can actually be MORE relaxed, MORE focused and MORE creative through mindfulness than through using drugs.

In some ways, this is a tough sell in our pill popping culture. Many are averse to putting effort into their mental wellbeing. However, one of the truths of the human condition is that anything worthwhile must be earned.

Simply apply your willpower, and you will advance with your mindfulness practices. As you advance you will begin to taste the fruit of freedom.

Use mindfulness to help you reduce your drug cravings. Be aware of where your mind is at when you are desiring to use. Take note of your obsessing mind chattering away. Learn to quiet this chatter down. Learn to "surf the urge" to reduce your cravings. Fully realize that the urge will crest and eventually diminish. Just ride the wave and attempt to control your unruly and obsessing mind. This is easier said than done but can be accomplished. You can learn to use mindfulness to assist you in finding moderation.

Another angle is to view drug addiction as a strong habit. Attempt to replace this habit with mindfulness practice. Use "mindfulness on the fly", (see chapter 4), as a substitute for substances. When you have put some time into your training, you will realize that you can achieve a **sustainable** elevated consciousness through mindfulness.

As we progress on the path of mindful awareness, we begin to develop an overall mindful perspective on our life and our reality. When this occurs, we begin to reap the rewards of focus, relaxation, synchronicity, joy and personal power throughout the day and night. This is the path of being naturally "high" through mindful living.

Freedom

From Excessive Anger
From Excessive Guilt
From Excessive Negative Self Talk

From an Overbearing Past
From the Fear of the Future

From Limiting Beliefs
From Judgments
From Various Addictions
From the Agitated Mind

Towards Inspiration
Towards Courage
Towards Fulfillment
Towards Moderation
Towards Peace of Mind

Freedom
To Think Clearly

To Be in the Zone
To Be in the Flow
!!!
!!

Chapter Three
Mindfulness Theory Basics

Finding Balance

The waking mind has essentially two modes of operation.

One of these modes is thinking or analysis. This can be viewed as the state of pondering the future or past, engaging in fantasy, or seeking intellectual understanding. This is the working state of the mind.

The second mode of operation is awareness/stillness. This state transcends the thinking state and is simply non-judgmental presence. This is the state of mindfulness. This is the resting state of mind.

Finding balance between these two mental modes is of the utmost importance for optimal mental functioning. When the thinking/awareness modes are in balance, the mind tends to be relaxed, clear and creative. However, when the analytical mode is dominant, the mind trends towards rigidity and agitation.

Overly active (compulsive) thinking is very prevalent in our modern culture. To be trapped in overthinking leads to being trapped in agitation. To be trapped in agitation is to be stuck in a self-made prison. Not surprisingly, finding balance in our mental processes is one key to mental health.

Balanced Thinking

Compulsive Thinking

thinking

awareness

Finding Flow

The flow state occurs when the mind is primarily in the awareness/stillness mode of operation. One key to being able to access this flow state regularly is to have a healthy balance between the thinking and awareness modes of mind throughout the day. Then, it is not such a big leap to access the flow state. However, if you are trapped in overthinking, then to achieve the flow state is difficult and may take extreme behavior such as engaging in some type of thrill sport to get there. It is therefore prudent for those of you who wish to access the flow state daily, to find balance in your day to day mind functioning.

This flow state can be viewed as a transcendental or peak experience.

$mmmm$ = thinking

_____ = awareness/
stillness

rumination $mmmmmmmmmmmmmmm$

balanced mmm——mmm——m—

flow state ————m————————

Finding Balance

Having Space
Between Thoughts
Is One Key
To Naturally and Effortlessly
Unlock
The Flow State

The Quality of Mind Continuum

The Quality of Mind Continuum (QMC) illustrates how the mind feels at any given moment. The mind is always somewhere on this continuum. It is useful to periodically refer to the QMC and determine approximately where your mind is at. This will enable you to be the pragmatic witness to your relationship between mindfulness and mental wellbeing.

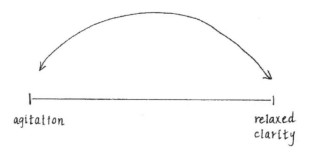

Many mental disorders/dysfunctions emanate from an agitated mind. Feelings of fear, anxiety, anger, and guilt spin out of the agitated perspective. When the agitated mind is worn out and needs a break, depression occurs. Conversely, positive feelings emanate from the state of relaxed clarity. Inspiration, deep understanding and a feeling of fulfillment emanate from this state.

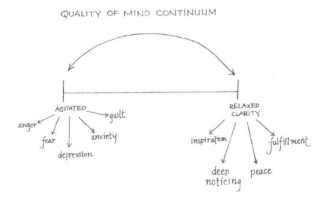

We each have a home base on this continuum.

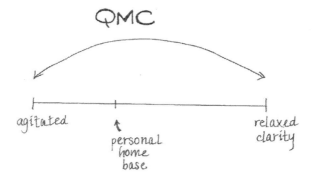

Through mindfulness practice we can move the home base of our mind towards relaxed clarity.

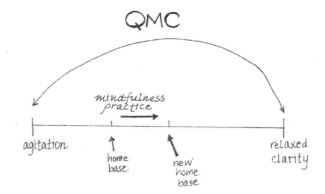

These simple diagrams illustrate *how* and *why* mindfulness promotes mental wellbeing.

Abraham Maslow

Maslow's "Hierarchy of Needs"
Identifies "Peak Experiences"
As a Regular Occurrence
For Those Who Are
"Self Actualized"

These "Peak Experiences"
Are Moments of Being in the
Flow

These "Peak Experiences"
Are Elongated Moments of
Mindfulness

Internal Processes

Being the Director of Your Mind

Step one to achieving a mindful perspective is to be the neutral observer of your own thoughts. To be mindful is to be the "empowered stillness" behind your conscious mind. From this perspective, you are able to accurately observe and direct your unique thinking patterns and habits.

Being the neutral observer of your thinking enables you to be the witness to how your mind operates. You will notice the various themes your mind trends towards, (the quality and type of thought) and how much your mind tends to think, (the quantity of thinking). You will also stop self-identifying with your thoughts. The end result of this is that instead of your thoughts controlling you, you will be the director of your thoughts.

Observing the quantity of your thoughts:

Do you think too much? Are you caught up in compulsive thinking? Do you find yourself ruminating over various difficulties and intrigues? Do you overthink? Does your mind find stillness periodically throughout the day? Does your mind quiet down easily at night? Do you sleep well?

Observing the quality of your thoughts:

Where does your mind trend? What does your mind habitually think about? Do your thoughts tend to be productive and focused? Is your thinking clear and relaxed?

Does your mind tend to be agitated and jump from thought to thought? How do you view yourself? What is the quality of your self-talk?

As we observe our own thoughts, we begin to notice certain patterns of thinking – i.e. familiar themes that we tend to gravitate towards. Some of these patterns are productive and healthy. However, some of the patterns are most likely unproductive and unhealthy.

Step two is to identify and label your unproductive thinking patterns. Some common unproductive patterns of thinking are "worst case scenario thinking," "negative self-talk" and "judgmental thinking." You should also be the witness of your thinking/awareness balance by noticing "compulsive thinking" and "rumination".

Step three is to disrupt unproductive thinking patterns. In doing so, you begin to condition your mind to be healthier and more productive. At this point you will begin to alter the energetic quality of your thinking. You will work with the specific content of your thoughts and your thinking/awareness balance. As you engage in disrupting old destructive and unbalanced thinking habits, your internal mental and emotional landscapes will change for the better. As you actively shift your thinking patterns, you will witness a positive shift in your self-esteem. You will naturally begin to feel more empowered over your mind and your circumstances.

How do I disrupt old unproductive patterns?

Use a mindfulness skill to "reboot" the mind (see chapter 4). Notice when your mind is caught up in a mental eddy and purposefully go into a mindful state to turn off or "reboot" the thought. Keep repeating this process until the old unproductive pattern doesn't surface into the conscious mind. Another technique is to re-steer destructive internal dialog. Notice when you are engaging in negative self-talk and replace this with more positive messages. As you engage in these processes, you will be training your mind. Eventually, old destructive patterns will be replaced by new productive mind habits.

As you progress, you will no longer be bound by old patterns of thought. You will be free from overthinking as well as old destructive thinking patterns. You will have found freedom. Your newfound liberation will empower you with **psychological resilience** and **vitality**. You will have achieved effective **emotional regulation** capabilities. You will have the clarity to fully understand your purpose and the tools to effectively navigate towards your goals. At this point, you are effectively liberated from old stuck patterns and are free to create the life that you are destined to live.

The Sixth Sense

Sharpen Your Five Senses
Hear the Birds
Smell the Flowers
Feel the Breeze
Taste the Food
See the Trees

Purely Connected
With the Moment

Then Take the Leap
To the Next Level
Of Awareness

Develop the Ability
To Witness
Your Habitual Thoughts

Shine the Light of Your Awareness
On Your Thought Processes

Be the Neutral Witness
To Your Internal Mindscape

Develop Your
Sixth Sense

Discernment Rather than Judgment

We live in a culture that is steeped with judgmental energy. From an early age, many of us are trained to blame others, look down on others, name-call others and in general to view the world through a judgmental lens. It is common to judge others as less than or better than us.

Judgement is a rigid perspective.

When we are discerning, we keep our minds open to see both the positive and negative aspects of any situation. Therefore, to be discerning is to have a free and inquiring state of mind. Conversely, judgmental thinking leads to a mind that is restrictive and narrow.

Attempt to view your life from an energetic perspective. To judge others, even if just in your thoughts, is to be energetically warring. For example, when I'm judging another person as being less than, I am energetically attacking this person. In contrast, when I'm viewing another through the lens of discernment, I am being the neutral witness to the other. That is not to say that discernment is a passive perspective. Just the opposite is true. If I am discerning, I am able to see any situation clearly and therefore am able to react appropriately.

It is also crucial to understand that if we are in the habit of judging others, we will also have the tendency to judge *ourselves*. Another way to see this is that the energy we put out into the world is reflected back at us. The habit of judgmental thinking can therefore be viewed as a self-destructive thinking habit. Self-judgment is extremely harmful to our self-esteem and overall confidence. Self-judgment reveals itself as negative self-talk, destructive behavior patterns and an overall sense of worthlessness and despair.

It is important for all of us to work against energetically attacking (judging) ourselves and others.

Once you break away from a judgmental perspective, *you will naturally feel better about your world and yourself.* It is a crucial component of a mindful lifestyle that will empower you to see clearly and behave accordingly. Do your best to become free from the shackles of judgment. See the world and yourself in the light of discernment and clarity. Attempt to free yourself from habitual judgmental thinking.

Momentum

Mind Patterns and Thinking Habits
Have their Own Momentum

To Alter
Their Trajectory

Requires

Watchfulness
Willpower

And
Effective Techniques

Seeking Gratitude

An attitude that accentuates mindfulness.

To be grateful for the moment is an effective method of achieving mindfulness. Attempt to cultivate an attitude of gratitude. Granted, being grateful is not always possible. When life is tough, this may be beyond our reach. However, when we can, it is wise and useful to cultivate this attitude.

Focus your mind on the joys that are naturally present: a beautiful sunset, a flower, a friend, a song, great food, and really take note of it. Focus on it, let yourself get lost in the moment, and feel grateful for it. Be thankful when the opportunity for gratitude presents itself.

The practice of gratitude also has the snowball effect. The more we are able to achieve gratitude, the more we will have to be grateful for. Get the ball rolling in the right direction and soon its momentum will carry us down the mindful path. Gratitude is a wondrous, pleasant, and profound gateway to mindfulness.

Gratitude

Walking Through the Parking Lot
I Hear the Birds Singing

I Say to Myself
"Thank You Universe for This Peaceful Moment"

Seeking Forgiveness

Forgiveness is a beneficial psychological trait.
Forgiveness is a skill. If you are unable to forgive, you
are anchored in the past. Forgiveness cuts the chain of
this anchor and allows you the freedom to more fully
experience the present.

From this perspective, being empowered to forgive
helps you to let go of events and people from your past
that no longer serve you. To forgive is an act of self-
compassion.

I am not suggesting forgiveness is easy. I am simply
suggesting that if you desire to forgive, you can move
with purpose in that direction.

Step one in forgiveness is to just say it. "I forgive
_____ for _____."

Even if you don't really mean it, this will get the
process started.

Step two is to use your discernment. Attempt to see
all sides of the issue.

Step three is to move into self-forgiveness. Self-
forgiveness is accentuated through discernment
because you are not caught in the rigid mindset of self-
judgment. You are able to see that the mistakes you've
made are part of the process of your personal growth
and not some permanent character flaw.

Step four is to work on these skills until they are a psychological habit. In other words, rewire your brain to be more forgiving to others and yourself.

Forgiveness and mindfulness have a strong relationship. Forgiveness is the process of letting go of some resentment or negative energy from the past. This letting go allows you to have more clarity in the moment. The more you can forgive (yourself and others), the more you can be alive and aware in the present moment. Forgiveness is an empowering skill that plays an important role in the mindful lifestyle.

It should be noted that to be forgiving in no way means for you to just accept abuse. Actually, the opposite is true. Forgiveness will empower you to become more present. This presence will in turn empower you to direct your life towards healthy circumstances. Ultimately, to be forgiving is to be clear-minded and powerful.

Your Personal Mantra

In our Minds We Talk to Ourselves
We Each Have Internal Dialog
This is Part of the Human Condition

To Engage in Habitual
Negative Self Talk
Is to Have a Negative Personal Mantra

This is very Detrimental to Your
Mental Wellbeing

Use Your Sixth Sense
(Be the Introspective Neutral Observer)
And Identify Your Self Talk

Shift Your Self Talk
Away from Negativity

"Everything Will Be All Right"
or
"We Are All Spiritual Beings"
or
"I Forgive Myself, I Did the Best I Could"

Are Examples of Self Talk
That May Counteract
Negative Self Talk
Consciously Develop
Positive Self Talk
As Your

Personal Mantra

Begin to Take Control
Of Your Internal Dialog

The Optimist/Realist/Pessimist Scale

In every situation, attempt to see both the positive and negative aspects. To see the entire picture enables you to act accordingly. The optimist sees only the good. The pessimist sees only the negative. The mindful realist sees the entire picture.

Another component of this scale is after viewing the entire picture, you can decide whether you want to put energy into changing the situation. If so, you must determine where to put your energy. I believe a solid strategy of change is to see the entirety of every situation. Then put energy into supporting the positive end of the scale. In other words, if you desire change, instead of fighting against the negative, it may be more effective to put energy into positive solutions.

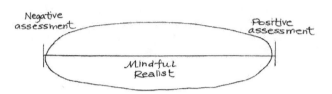

Chapter Four

- Practices –

Taking on the Dragon

Learning to Meditate

There are many ways to be in the moment. For example, awareness can be achieved through activities like moving, dancing, walking, playing, and making art. However, sitting meditation is a practice that helps to accentuate all other mindfulness practices. During sitting meditation, it's just you and your thoughts. Old patterns of thought will attempt to dominate your thinking. If you take on the challenge of a sitting mindfulness practice, you will most likely experience a raging internal battle. Stay with this and notice what is going on. Begin to be the "mind behind the mind" and see if you can begin to witness your thinking from a neutral perspective. Try to stay with this and persevere. Attempt to identify with the stillness behind your thoughts. This perspective will bring you great peace and a deep understanding of yourself and others.

Perhaps as you read this, old unproductive patterns of thought will say to you, "I can't meditate," or "I don't want to meditate," or "I'm above this," or "What a drag, I'll be bored." However, if you can overcome this unproductive thinking and apply your will towards a sitting mediation practice, you will be amazed at the results. For beginners, I suggest 10 minutes a day. Sit and find stillness. Even a few seconds of stillness are vastly beneficial for your mental health. Most likely, your mind will refuse to be present most of the time. If you want to find more stillness, increase your moment to moment awareness by focusing on postural and breath awareness. Persevere. Find freedom from the chattering mind.

Remember that every time you are able to find stillness, you are promoting your personal mental wellness. As you do this, you will be empowering yourself to steer your life in the direction of your dreams. Meditation builds power and energy. It truly is taking on the dragon…

The Challenge

Words can only Point
To the Direction

True Knowledge
Can Only be Attained

Through Awareness
Quietude
Stillness
Oneness

Practical Mindfulness Tips – Mindfulness on the Fly -

Mindfulness Tip 1: Metacognition, a Mindful Perspective – Develop Your Sixth Sense

Be the neutral observer of your thoughts. Take a step back from your thinking and be the "mind behind the mind." View your world and your mind from the perspective of "empowered stillness". From this powerful perspective, you will be able to be the director of your thinking processes. Instead of your thoughts directing you, you will be able to direct your thoughts! This is an empowering perspective that you can take with you wherever you are.

Mindfulness Tip 2: Focus Words

Quieting the mental internal chatter is a crucial component of mindful living. Using "focus words" can be a highly effective method to accomplish this task. When the mental chatter is out of balance, (stuck in rumination or highly negative), using "focus words" can bring back a clear and healthy mental landscape. To practice this skill, breath in and say in your mind, "Sooooooo." While exhaling, say in your mind, "Hummmmm."

Try it now for one breath. Inhale – "Soooooooo" Exhale – "Hummmmm". These "focus words" can effectively blot out unproductive mental chatter. This is rebooting your mind. If this practice resonates with you, use it throughout the day. "Focus words" are a powerful mindfulness cultivation tool that enable you to steer your mind into a place of balance and clarity. You can also use these focus words while sitting in meditation or at night to quiet the agitated mind and promote deep sleep.

Mindfulness Tip 3: Walk in the Present Tense

Being mindful while walking is a practical, simple, and profound practice. Attempt to be fully present while moving about. Focus on posture, fluid movement, and being fully aware of what you see, hear and feel.

You can also coordinate your breathing with your steps. A tricky yet very effective mindfulness hack is to take five steps while inhaling, five steps while exhaling. Add some focus words to the mix and you will have a tremendous mindfulness cultivation skill that you can use many times a day. It will take some time to master this technique, but it is well worth the effort. A disclaimer for this practice - make sure you are aware of your surroundings when you are practicing mindful walking!

Mindfulness Tip 4: Optimal Standing, Posture and Movement

This is a very utilitarian practice that can be used many times a day. In fact, by learning optimal standing you will be both learning a very amazing mindfulness skill plus promoting hip, knee, and back health. This mindfulness hack can also be particularly helpful in stressful social situations. For those who suffer from social anxiety, this is a great exercise.

Let your head be pulled up from above. Your knees are soft – weight equally distributed between the feet. Imagine your feet are rooted into the ground. Your shoulders are back and down. Your breathing is full and your eyes are clear. Be in a place of relaxed-clarity and balance.

Practice postural awareness as you sit as well. Be mindful of what your posture is like and how your posture relates to how you are feeling. Good posture often translates into confidence and awareness.

Also, be aware of how you are moving. To the best of your ability, keep your movements fluid and circular. Try to remain in a state of relaxed strength and balance. Tai Chi training is an effective method for working on optimal standing, posture, and movement.

Mindfulness Tip 5: Relaxation Breath

Through paying attention to your breath, you will begin to see the relationship between the quality of breath and how you feel. Shallow breathing tends to create stress and agitation in the mind. To counteract shallow breathing, focus on fully exhaling. Realize that the complete and relaxed full exhalation is an important component of optimal breathing. Slowly breath out all the way. Empty your lungs then allow the lungs to fully inflate. Focus on your lungs moving as gracefully as possible. Do not hold your breath between inhalation and exhalation. Paying attention to your exhalation is a great tool to assist you in becoming focused, centered and relaxed.

Mindfulness Tip 6: Power Breathing

This type of breathing builds power and vigor. Have good posture. Attempt to fill the lungs from the bottom to the top, as you inhale. Feel you ribs expand underneath your armpits. Feel your ribs in your back expand, as well. Remain in a place of relaxed strength and balance. Let your body exhale fully and naturally. As you near the end of your exhalation, activate your abdominal muscles and pull in your stomach. At the beginning of your inhalation, let your stomach expand slightly, then expand your ribs. Continue with this pattern. Do not hold your breath between inhalation and exhalation.

Power breathing energizes, as it bathes your brain and muscles in oxygen. Power breathing also strengthens the abdominals. Personally, I like to use power breathing as much as possible. It is a great practice for hiking in the mountains, sitting at your desk, or while engaging in tantric union.

Mindfulness Tip 7: Five-Seven-Ten Breathing

This tip utilizes a modern version of bamboo breathing from the Zen tradition. To begin, breath in all the way in a relaxed manner. As you exhale segment your breath into five sections. (Segment your breathing by stopping and starting the flow of air). Inhale again – then breath out in seven segments. Breathe in again and now exhale in ten segments. End by taking one deep inhalation and exhalation. This tip is useful when the mind is particularly agitated and needs to be reined in.

Mindfulness Tip 8: Subtle Breathing

Quiet the breathing. Let your lungs move as gracefully as possible. Let the breathing be as soft as possible. Notice that as you make your breath subtle, the mind also relaxes. This can be an effective method at reducing or eliminating headaches. This type of breathing can also be a great way to inducing a quiet mind while engaging in sitting meditation. Subtle breathing combined with focus words are also an effective strategy to induce sleep.

Through paying attention to your breath, you will begin to witness the relationship between the quality of your breath and how you feel. Shallow and agitated breathing tends to create stress and agitation in the mind. These four breathing techniques are empowering and practical mindfulness life hacks.

Mindfulness Tip 9: Mindful Interpersonal Interactions

Be as present as possible during interpersonal interactions. This means be a great listener. Let go of the idea that it is your role be the advisor. Let go of the philosophy that some people are below you. Let go of judgement and arrogance.

Remember that arrogance is based on the self-delusion that you are intrinsically superior to others. Realize that everyone has something to offer you, that everyone has some wisdom to share.

View interpersonal interactions from an energetic perspective. Attempt to raise your vibration as high as possible and realize that you can profoundly benefit another through simply emanating positive/aware/clear energy. Know that it is possible to walk into a room full of people and shift the energy without even saying a word. Have fun with this reality.

As far as verbal communication, develop the habit of allowing your voice to be relaxed and clear. Let your conversations be purposeful. Avoid name-calling or micro aggressions (judgmental or condescending talk). Be aware of both your vocal quality and the intended purpose of your conversations.

Also, try to eliminate the habit of mean spirited gossiping. Understand that if you engage in mean spirited gossip, you are creating negative energy that in some way will be reflected back at you.

"Preach Incessantly
Use Words
Only When Necessary"

- *Saint Francis of Assisi*

Mindfulness Tip 10: Develop a New Relationship with Food

The sun plays a significant role in all food. It energizes the plants that provide food for us all. The sun is, in fact, the source of the energy that we ingest when we are eating. An exercise we can use while eating is visualizing the connection our food has with the sun. We combine this visualization with mindfully seeing, touching, smelling, hearing, and tasting the food we are eating.

For example, when eating a piece of broccoli, first imagine it sitting in a field soaking up the energy of the sun. Then mindfully eat the broccoli, experiencing it with all of your senses. When eating a piece of meat, imagine the animal standing in the sun and eating grain that has been soaking up the sun's energy. Then mindfully proceed with eating. Chewing your food completely and not over-eating are also part of mindful eating experience.

To practice this type of mindful eating is to respect the relationship between the food we eat, the sun, and ourselves. It is reverent and grounding. Try to incorporate mindful eating at least once a day with either a full meal or a snack. Use these techniques more often if it is helpful for you.

Mindfulness Tip 11: Drum in the 5/4

This tip is effective for those who are musically inclined. It is drumming to the 5/4-time signature. This is an esoteric rhythm that promotes present moment awareness. Musically speaking, we are not used to hearing the 5/4. It therefore stuns the conscious mind because it is unusual to our ear. The 5/4 can be viewed as a rhythmic zen koan.

To drum this esoteric rhythm takes extreme focus. Drumming the 5/4 promotes present moment awareness. To learn more about esoteric rhythms and drumming the 5/4 visit our website at www.IMI.earth

Also, listening to music in 5/4 is great way to familiarize your mind with this esoteric rhythm. Some bands that play some songs in 5/4 are Radiohead, Dave Brubeck and Lotus Head.

Mindfulness Tip 12: Understand the Ratchet Effect

Two steps forward and one step back. Then two steps forward and another step back. Two more steps forward... This "ratchet effect" is the natural rhythm of progress. Know that when you have that "one step back" day, it's okay. It is the natural way of progress, so don't be hard on yourself. When you have that "one step back day', label it a ratchet day and move on with your life.

Mindfulness Tip 13: Reframe Anxiety

It seems to be therapeutically beneficial to reframe "anxiety" as "agitation". Anxiety is difficult to work against because it is an emotional experience that has vague origins. It is very prevalent in our culture yet not well understood. The term "anxiety attack" evokes a feeling of being attacked by some amorphous force. How do we possibly defend ourselves against such an attack?

Replace the term "anxiety attack" with "agitation attack". Now, you can have a solid strategy of how to counter this experience through finding relaxed clarity. This leads to confidence in your ability to effectively deal with anxiety/agitation.

Mindfulness Tip 14: Honor Your Mind

Attempt to view your mind as a great and powerful tool that has the latent ability to vastly improve your life. Honor this reality by taking good care of your mind. Earnestly work with your "mental diet". Earnestly work against judgment and negative self-talk. Earnestly work against rumination and compulsive thinking. Earnestly find stillness as much as possible to empower your innate cognitive abilities.

■■■

These fourteen mindfulness tips can be used as a form of preventative mental health and crisis intervention. Attempt to be in the habit of using these skills periodically throughout the day and night. By incorporating these skills into your day-to-day living, you build great emotional resilience. Life, in general, will feel lighter as your mind will be much more relaxed and clear.

Also, when a crisis occurs, you will have a variety of well-rehearsed mindfulness skills at your disposal. From this perspective, a crisis can be seen as an opportunity to test your mindfulness metal. Can you remain balanced, relaxed and clear in the face of a crisis? Or will you spin off into agitation? If you go into agitation, can you come back to relaxed clarity relatively quickly? Life will no doubt bring you opportunities to test your mindfulness abilities. As you begin to pass these tests, you will be in a powerful position to be the effective director of your life.

See www.IMI.earth for more detailed instructions on these utilitarian mindfulness tips!

Cultivating Awareness

Feed Your Mind Conscientiously
(Have a Healthy Mental Diet)

Train Your Mind Effectively
(Regularly Engage in Mindful Practices)

Develop Your Sixth Sense
(Learn to be the Neutral Witness to Your Thoughts)

Be the Director of Your Thinking
(Learn to Reboot and Steer Your Thoughts)

Rest Your Mind
(Learn to Find Stillness)

The Habit of Mindful Living is Transformative

As we learn to become more mindful, a series of developmental quantum leaps will likely occur. They are as follows:

We feel empowered.

Our self-esteem increases.

We begin to see the good in ourselves and in our world.

We begin to distance ourselves from enervating and negative situations.

We become more trusting in our intuitive nature.

We learn to be more forgiving of others and ourselves.

We reduce the habit of blaming others for our circumstances.

We feel that the universe is on our side.

Our lives begin to feel lighter and more joyous.

Our individual purpose becomes clear to us.

We begin to be the change that we want to see in the world.

This process of awakening to clarity is not without its challenges. Staying the course through tough times is a test that each of us will most likely face. However, an exciting life awaits those who undertake this quest. Mindful living is indeed a way of being that is conducive to adventure and progress.

The Ascending Cycle of Mindful Living

As you become more mindful, you are naturally rewarded. As you begin to put more positive constructive energy out into the world, positive energy will begin to come back to you. As you walk the walk of a mindful lifestyle, you will notice that life has many positive surprises in store for you. What awaits you? Develop an overall mindful perspective and find out. Indeed, life is a great adventure.

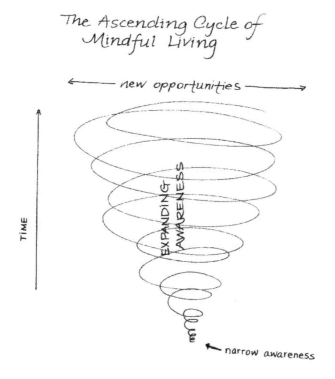

The Ascending Cycle of Mindful Living

← — new opportunities — →

TIME

EXPANDING AWARENESS

← narrow awareness

Chapter Five

Ethics

A Note to Mental Health Therapists

Please, learn mindfulness yourself before attempting to share it with your clients. Refer out if need be. I've witnessed clients who were turned off to the mindfulness experience because they were "trained" by therapists who didn't really understand it themselves. If you want to share this art, you must first know it. To "know" mindfulness, you must be a regular practitioner of it. This "knowing" is beyond intellectual understanding. It is a feeling you achieve through your mindfulness practice.

To effectively use mindfulness therapeutically, you need to have acquired some level of expertise in it yourself. For example, a person who doesn't play the violin would make a dismal violin teacher. This same paradigm is true for mindfulness. If you are interested in helping your clients with mindfulness techniques, step one is to train yourself. To ethically and therapeutically be able to use mindfulness for your clients, first walk the walk.

The Three Stages of Mindfulness Attainment

There are three basic stages of mindfulness attainment.

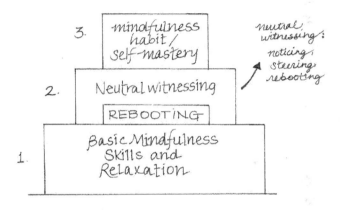

THREE STAGES OF MINDFULNESS ATTAINMENT

3. mindfulness habit / self-mastery

2. Neutral witnessing

REBOOTING

1. Basic Mindfulness Skills and Relaxation

neutral witnessing: noticing, steering, rebooting

Stage One

We attain the ability of basic relaxation. In this stage, we can usually calm our mind down at will by practicing a mindfulness skill.

Stage Two

In this stage, we work on being the discerning observer of our thinking processes. We begin to identify both productive and destructive thinking patterns. We then learn to apply our mindfulness skills to disrupt unproductive thinking patterns, thereby replacing them with productive mental habits.

Stage two is the hard-working stage of mindfulness attainment. In stage two, we are actively engaged in rewiring our brains.

Stage Three

The overall mindful perspective is habitual. New productive patterns of thinking have been installed and habitually occur. At this point, we have effectively reprogramed our thinking patterns. Our minds are resilient and balanced. This is the stage of freedom.

I believe that to effectively use mindfulness therapeutically, you need to be personally engaged in stage two or three of mindfulness attainment.

Chapter Six
Psychological Challenges

Depression and anxiety run rampant in our culture. On top of this, many of us are dealing with trauma and also have a variety of other emotional difficulties. This chapter is designed to illustrate how and why mindfulness naturally counteracts psychological dysfunction. Mindfulness can be used in conjunction with more traditional therapeutic techniques to "supercharge" the healing process. I've chosen to exclusively use the unconventional writing method of "informational poetry" for this section of the book because it gets straight to the point – it cuts to the chase of what I'm attempting to illuminate. Please, take your time in reading and "digesting" these brief informational poems.

R.A.M.

The
Relentless Agitated Mind
Is An
Internal Prison Sentence

It is an Extreme Case of Mental Agitation
It Disrupts Sleep
It Makes Clear Thought Virtually Impossible

To be Trapped in Agitation
Is to Be Stuck
in Gnawing Emotional Pain

R.A.M.
Can Lead to
Suicidal Ideation

Free Yourself From the Shackles
Of R.A.M.

Through Mindful Living

Anxiety

Mental Agitation is the Root
Of Anxiety

Therefore
Learning to Overcome

Or Reduce
Mental Agitation

Strikes at the Roots
Of Anxiety

Reframe

Attempt to Rename

"Anxiety Attacks"
As
"Agitation Attacks"

This Will Put You in a Position
To Effectively Counteract
This Common Dysfunction

Mindfulness to Reduce Social Anxiety

In Social Situations
Practice Mindful Posture and Movement

also
Be the Mindful Observer of Others

also
Do Mindful Walking
As You Approach the Social Event

Through Training in These 3 Mindfulness Skills

You Will Be Empowered Over Your
Social Anxiety

Social Anxiety 2 – Being the Mindful Observer

At a Work Meeting
Sitting Around a Table Full of People

Notice How the *Other* People
Are Feeling
Mindfully Notice the *Other* Peoples' Energy

Be the Energetic Observer
Of the Situation

Realize
That if You Can Maintain a High Level
Of Mindfulness

You Will
Help Yourself
And All the Others in the Room
Feel better

Practice This
In All Social Situations

Find Meaning

Get in Touch
With Your Purpose
Create Meaning
In Your Life
Move with Purpose
Down Your Path

Courage and Inspiration
Naturally Evolve
Through Meaningful Living

Depression

The Agitated Mind
Exhausts Itself
Through Constant Internal Chattering
And Jumping Around

Needing a Break
From its' State of
Monkey Mind

The Agitated Mind
Wears Out

And Sinks into the Place
Of Depression

Mindfulness Trauma Reduction

When Traumatic Thoughts
Bubble Up
From the Subconscious Mind
Into the Conscious mind

Meet Them
From a Place of Equanimity
And Emotional Balance

Use Your Mindfulness Training
To Be the Neutral Observer
The Discerning Observer
The Non-Judgmental Observer
Of These Traumatic Thoughts

Notice These Thoughts Clearly and Calmly
And then Release Them
To the Universe

Anger Management

We All Become Upset
However

Mindful Individuals
Are Able
To
Get back to Center More Quickly

Thereby
Creating less Damage
In Their
Lives

Mindfulness Empowers Us
To
1. Identify Our Mental Agitation
then
2. To Reboot our Thoughts

Ruminating on Upsetting Events

Feeds the Fire
Of
The Angry Mind

Finding Stillness
During the Storm
Is a Valuable Skill

Chapter Seven
For the Spiritually Inclined

For those of you readers who are spiritually inclined, you may wish to consider the possibility of "soulful awareness" as a mindfulness practice. From this perspective, we are spiritual beings having a temporary human experience. This viewpoint allows us to take a step back from all the worries and drama of our existence. From this perspective, we understand that one hundred years goes by like a flash of lightening and "reality" is mystical indeed. "Soulful awareness" also reveals to us the basic and profound connection we have with other people and the universe itself. In fact, this perspective is the destroyer of prejudice, arrogance and fear. Truly, to taste the fruit of "soulful awareness" is to experience a vital and wondrous state of being.

Soulful Awareness Mindfulness Practice

Step 1.
Slightly Deepen the Breath
Check Your Posture
Be in a State of Relaxed Strength

Step 2.
Visualize
A Spark of Intense Light
Inside Your Body
Residing Behind
Your Solar Plexus

See This Light As Your Soul

Step 3.
Begin to See
This Spark of Light In Others

And Realize
We Are All
Soulful Beings

Develop Soulful Awareness
As a Habit
And Behold the Joy
Of
Peace Of Mind

A Contemporary Mystic

Thomas Merton
Catholic Monk and Contemporary
Mystic

Believed That the Higher Power
Is a Force

That Is Always Attempting to
Connect with Us

Perhaps the Tumultuous Mind
Blocks This Energy

Perhaps the Still Mind
Allows This Universal Energy
To Reside Within Us

The New Transcendentalism

Beyond Words We View the Moment
Connected to the Present
In Touch with Reality

In Conclusion: A Note to the Reader

We are all wildly powerful manifestors. This is our birthright. One way of viewing humankind is that we are mystical beings who are unaware of our latent manifesting abilities. Ignorant of our power, we wander around the earth creating both horror and beauty depending on our collective mind states. Since our super human (manifesting) abilities are mostly unknown to us, we do not respect the power of our own minds. We usually don't take our "mental diets" into account. We have the tendency to engage in compulsive over thinking and many of us are judgmental.

Overall, this creates an agitated mindset, which in turn creates disharmonious circumstances. As humanity begins to mature, we will learn more and more about our innate abilities. However, for now, attempt to understand the importance of the moment. Attempt to take responsibility for your thoughts and work on improving your culture in an organic and fruitful way – starting with improving your own mind.

As you begin to tread on this path, life will become wondrous and fulfilling. This is the evolution of humankind and is our collective destiny.

Chapter Eight

Hosting a Mindfulness Meetup Group

Do you want to be a mindfulness leader in your community?

If so, I suggest considering starting a donation based mindfulness meetup group. Build community! Improve your Karma! Make some $!

1. Become proficient at mindfulness. Train yourself. Practice sitting daily. Perhaps take a Tai Chi Class, do some gentle yoga, or check out a Zen or other meditation center. Be proactive about learning the art of mindfulness. Work with your mind. Incorporate the "Practical Mindfulness Tips" into your life. Take the step into Mindful Living.

2. Find a free space in which you can lead this group. Some potential examples: your co-op, a church, your apartment etc.

3. Advertise! Facebook, posters, community radio etc.

4. Accept donations.

5. Use this book as a workbook – encourage each member to have their own copy.

Set a date and begin a new chapter of your life as a mindfulness advocate and educator!

www.IMI.earth

Please reread this book.

Chapter Nine
Mindfulness
Workbook

Using this workbook:

This workbook is designed to assist the reader in developing an overall mindful perspective. It can be used by groups or individuals. Attempt to fill out this worksheet regularly.

For "Mindfulness Meetup Groups," I suggest beginning the group with a ten-minute sitting mindfulness practice. Then go around the group and discuss various questions from the worksheet. End the group by having another short meditation.

This Workbook

Might Be
A Gateway

Into a Great Adventure

Enjoy the Process
Of Looking Deeply Within

mindfulness – Non-judgmental Awareness
(a recap)

1. Finding balance between thinking
   and awareness.

   ~~~~~~~~~   ~~~~~~   ~~~~~   ~~~~~.   ~~~

2. The Quality of Mind Continuum (QMC)

   AGITATION   RELAXED
                                          CLARITY

3. Reality Scale

   NEGATIVE   POSITIVE
   ASSESSMENT   ASSESSMENT

4. Training
   Various Practices
     meditation, yoga, tai chi,
     mantra, nature walks ...

Mindful Lifestyle – A Recap

Mental Diet
Utilitarian Practices
Introspection
Identifying old patterns of thought
Rebooting Re-steering
Finding space between thoughts
Creating Balance
Promoting Discernment over Judgement
Promoting Gratitude
Promoting Forgiveness
Finding Peace Through Presence

Note from Jai

The following workbook suggestion: Please take time each day to fill out some or all of the worksheet in your own notebook. Keep a journal of your progress! Create momentum in your mindful lifestyle by taking note of the process for 30 days in a row. It is ok to start over when you need to. It's a game. Go on and play!

You can also copy/scan, print and share the following worksheets with your mindfulness meetup community.

Be Mindful

Workbook

WORKSHEET

1. Describe your mental diet over the last 24 hours.

2. Place your needle on the QMC for this moment.

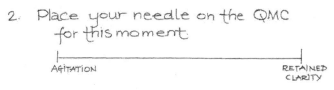

AGITATION   RETAINED CLARITY

3. Fill in your Reality Scale for the last 24 hours.

NEGATIVE ASSESSMENT   POSITIVE ASSESSMENT

4. Describe your mindfulness training over the last 24 hours.

5. How did you sleep last night?
   Scale of 1 (agitated) - 10 (relaxed) _____

6. Did you identify unproductive thinking patterns? _____

7. Did you successfully reboot an unproductive thinking pattern? _____

WORKSHEET

1. Describe your mental diet over the last 24 hours.

2. Place your needle on the QMC for this moment.

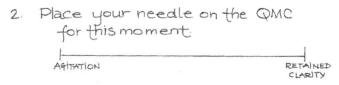

AGITATION   RETAINED CLARITY

3. Fill in your Reality Scale for the last 24 hours.

NEGATIVE ASSESSMENT   POSITIVE ASSESSMENT

4. Describe your mindfulness training over the last 24 hours.

5. How did you sleep last night? Scale of 1 (agitated) - 10 (relaxed) _____

6. Did you identify unproductive thinking patterns? _____

7. Did you successfully reboot an unproductive thinking pattern? _____

Workbook

WORKSHEET

1. Describe your mental diet over the last 24 hours.

2. Place your needle on the QMC for this moment

AGITATION   RETAINED CLARITY

3. Fill in your Reality Scale for the last 24 hours.

NEGATIVE ASSESSMENT   POSITIVE ASSESSMENT

4. Describe your mindfulness training over the last 24 hours.

5. How did you sleep last night? Scale of 1 (agitated) - 10 (relaxed) _____

6. Did you identify unproductive thinking patterns? _____

7. Did you successfully reboot an unproductive thinking pattern? _____

Workbook

WORKSHEET

1. Describe your mental diet over the last 24 hours.

2. Place your needle on the QMC for this moment.

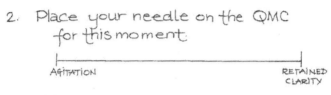

AGITATION   RETAINED CLARITY

3. Fill in your Reality Scale for the last 24 hours.

NEGATIVE ASSESSMENT   POSITIVE ASSESSMENT

4. Describe your mindfulness training over the last 24 hours.

5. How did you sleep last night? Scale of 1 (agitated) - 10 (relaxed) _____

6. Did you identify unproductive thinking patterns? _____

7. Did you successfully reboot an unproductive thinking pattern? _____

WORKSHEET

1. Describe your mental diet over the last 24 hours.

2. Place your needle on the QMC for this moment.

|————————————————————————————|

AGITATION   RETAINED
                                                        CLARITY

3. Fill in your Reality Scale for the last 24 hours.

|————————————————————————————|

NEGATIVE   POSITIVE
ASSESSMENT   ASSESSMENT

4. Describe your mindfulness training over the last 24 hours.

5. How did you sleep last night?
   Scale of 1 (agitated) - 10 (relaxed) _____

6. Did you identify unproductive thinking patterns? _____

7. Did you successfully reboot an unproductive thinking pattern? _____

WORKSHEET

1. Describe your mental diet over the last 24 hours.

2. Place your needle on the QMC for this moment.

AGITATION   RETAINED CLARITY

3. Fill in your Reality Scale for the last 24 hours.

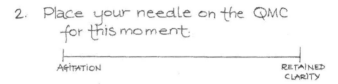

NEGATIVE ASSESSMENT   POSITIVE ASSESSMENT

4. Describe your mindfulness training over the last 24 hours.

5. How did you sleep last night?
   Scale of 1 (agitated) - 10 (relaxed) _____

6. Did you identify unproductive thinking patterns? _____

7. Did you successfully reboot an unproductive thinking pattern? _____

WORKSHEET

1. Describe your mental diet over the last 24 hours.

2. Place your needle on the QMC for this moment.

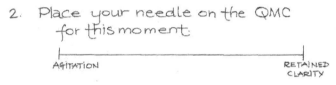

AGITATION   RETAINED CLARITY

3. Fill in your Reality Scale for the last 24 hours.

NEGATIVE   POSITIVE
ASSESSMENT   ASSESSMENT

4. Describe your mindfulness training over the last 24 hours.

5. How did you sleep last night?
   Scale of 1 (agitated) - 10 (relaxed) _____

6. Did you identify unproductive thinking patterns? _____

7. Did you successfully reboot an unproductive thinking pattern? _____

Workbook

WORKSHEET

1. Describe your mental diet over the last 24 hours.

2. Place your needle on the QMC for this moment.

|————————————————————————————|
AGITATION   RETAINED CLARITY

3. Fill in your Reality Scale for the last 24 hours.

|————————————————————————————|
NEGATIVE ASSESSMENT   POSITIVE ASSESSMENT

4. Describe your mindfulness training over the last 24 hours.

5. How did you sleep last night? Scale of 1 (agitated) - 10 (relaxed) _____

6. Did you identify unproductive thinking patterns? _____

7. Did you successfully reboot an unproductive thinking pattern? _____

WORKSHEET

1. Describe your mental diet over the last 24 hours.

2. Place your needle on the QMC for this moment.

AGITATION   RETAINED CLARITY

3. Fill in your Reality Scale for the last 24 hours.

NEGATIVE ASSESSMENT   POSITIVE ASSESSMENT

4. Describe your mindfulness training over the last 24 hours.

5. How did you sleep last night? Scale of 1 (agitated) - 10 (relaxed) _____

6. Did you identify unproductive thinking patterns? _____

7. Did you successfully reboot an unproductive thinking pattern? _____

WORKSHEET

1. Describe your mental diet over the last 24 hours.

2. Place your needle on the QMC for this moment.

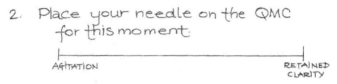

AGITATION   RETAINED
                                            CLARITY

3. Fill in your Reality Scale for the last 24 hours.

NEGATIVE   POSITIVE
ASSESSMENT   ASSESSMENT

4. Describe your mindfulness training over the last 24 hours.

5. How did you sleep last night?
   Scale of 1 (agitated) - 10 (relaxed) _____

6. Did you identify unproductive thinking patterns? _____

7. Did you successfully reboot an unproductive thinking pattern? _____

Workbook

WORKSHEET

1. Describe your mental diet over the last 24 hours.

2. Place your needle on the QMC for this moment.

|————————————————————————————|
AGITATION   RETAINED
                                             CLARITY

3. Fill in your Reality Scale for the last 24 hours.

|————————————————————————————|
NEGATIVE   POSITIVE
ASSESSMENT   ASSESSMENT

4. Describe your mindfulness training over the last 24 hours.

5. How did you sleep last night?
   Scale of 1 (agitated) - 10 (relaxed) _____

6. Did you identify unproductive thinking patterns? _____

7. Did you successfully reboot an unproductive thinking pattern? _____

68022137R00076

Made in the USA
Columbia, SC
03 August 2019